VOCAL • PIANO

ANDY WILLIAMS

ORIGINAL KEYS FOR SINGERS

Cover photo courtesy of Henry Mancini Enterprises, Inc.

ISBN 978-1-4234-9641-0

HAL•LEONARD®
CORPORATION
7777 W. BLUEMOUND RD. P.O. BOX 13819 MILWAUKEE, WI 53213

Visit Hal Leonard Online at
www.halleonard.com

ANDY WILLIAMS

Andy Williams began his amazing career in his hometown of Wall Lake, Iowa. It was there he started singing with his three brothers in a local Presbyterian church choir established by his parents. At the tender age of 8, Andy made his professional singing debut as part of the Williams Brothers Quartet. The brothers became regulars on radio station WHO's "Iowa's Barn Dance Show" in Des Moines, Iowa. From there the brothers continued to be featured prominently on national stations like WLS in Chicago and WLW in Cincinnati. The widespread radio exposure brought the brothers a considerable following which eventually caught the attention of Bing Crosby. With Crosby, Andy and his brothers made their first professional recording, "Swinging on a Star," which became a tremendous hit in 1944.

In 1947, Andy and his brothers teamed up with comedienne Kay Thompson (author of the popular children's book series *Eloise*) for a successful, trend setting nightclub act. Thompson and the brothers spent the next few years performing all over the U.S. and in London, but it came to an end in 1951 as the group disbanded and each brother went his own way. Andy chose to move to New York to pursue his vocal career.

While in New York, Andy became a regular performer on Steve Allen's *Tonight Show*, which led to his first recording contract with Cadence Records. It wasn't long before Andy had his first Top 10 hit with "Canadian Sunset." A string of hits followed, including "Butterfly," "Lonely Street," "Village of St. Bernadette," and "The Hawaiian Wedding Song," for which he received the first of his five GRAMMY® Award nominations.

His work in television continued with regular guest appearances on the Dinah Shore and Perry Como shows, and in 1958 he presented *The Chevy Showroom with Andy Williams*. In the summer of 1959, Andy was chosen by CBS to host a variety program replacing *The Gary Moore Show* for a thirteen-week period. When this series of shows concluded, Andy began to concentrate on one-hour television specials. The first, "Music from Schubert Alley," was presented by NBC on November 13, 1959.

A change in recording labels kicked Andy's career into high gear when he began his 25-year association with Columbia Records in 1962. Almost immediately he scored his first Top 10 hit for Columbia, "Can't Get Used to Losing You." Many more hits followed, but none would become more associated with Andy Williams than "Moon River," the Oscar-winning song from the film *Breakfast at Tiffany's*. This song became his theme song and propelled the album, *Moon River and Other Great Movie Themes* to the top of the charts. The following year Andy released the album *Days of Wine and Roses*, which spent an incredible sixteen weeks at #1 and stayed on the charts for over 100 weeks. His subsequent recordings were best sellers and resulted in eighteen gold and three platinum-certified albums.

Williams became a superstar after the debut of his weekly television series on NBC, *The Andy Williams Show*. His new variety show was seen for the first time on September 16, 1962, and ran for nine years, winning three Emmy Awards for Best Musical/Variety Series (1966, 1967, and 1969). It was one of NBC's top-rated programs and helped launch his classic Christmas specials featuring the entire Williams family.

Live performances continued to be a big part of Andy's career, and in 1966 he opened at Caesar's Palace and subsequently headlined at the famed Las Vegas hotel for the next twenty years. By the time *The Andy Williams Show* ended in 1972, Andy had become a true international superstar. With tremendous world-wide record sales and global distribution of his television show, he is just as popular in other countries as he is in the United States. This recognition prompted several tours of England, Europe, Australia, Japan, and Asia, breaking attendance records wherever he appeared. Andy currently performs at the *Andy Williams Moon River Theater* in Branson, Missouri, where he continues to present his live Variety and award-winning Christmas shows.

ARE YOU SINCERE

Words and Music by WAYNE WALKER
and LUCKY MOELLER

Moderately slow 12/8 feel

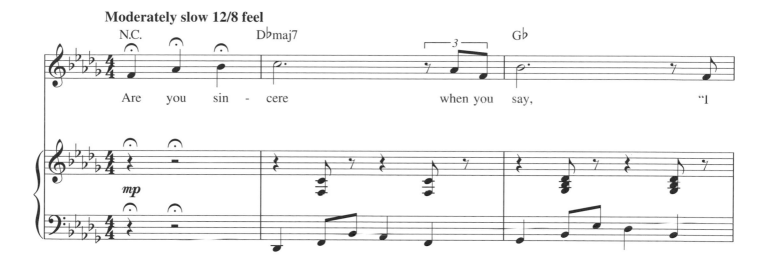

Are you sin-cere when you say, "I

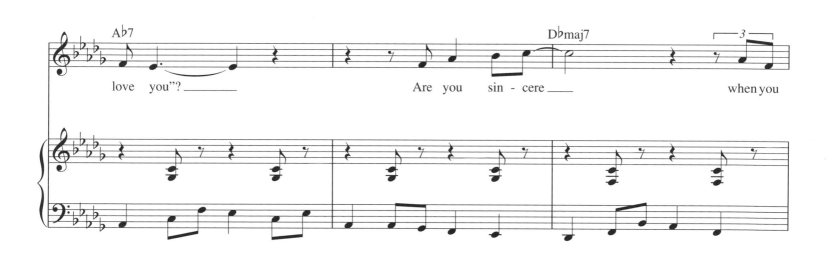

love you"? Are you sin-cere when you

say, "I'll be true"? Do you

BUTTERFLY

Words and Music by KAL MANN
and BERNIE LOWE

Moderately fast

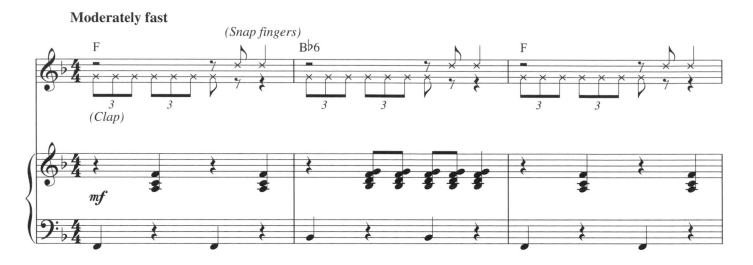

You tell me you love __ me, you
treat - in' me mean; _____ you're

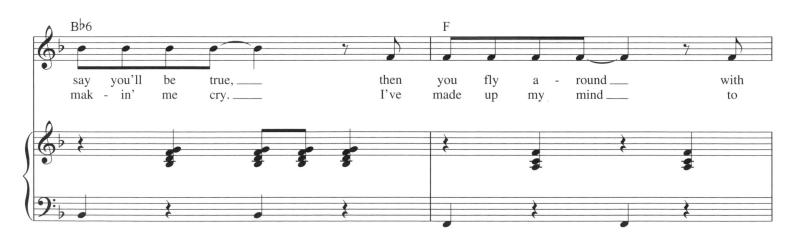

say you'll be true, ___ then you fly a - round __ with
mak - in' me cry. ___ I've made up my mind __ to

you but - ter - fly. _____

(Snap fingers)
(Clap)

Ooh, I'm cra - zy a - bout ___ you, ___ you but - ter -

- fly. _____

you but - ter - fly. _

CAN'T GET USED TO LOSING YOU

Words and Music by DOC POMUS
and MORT SHUMAN

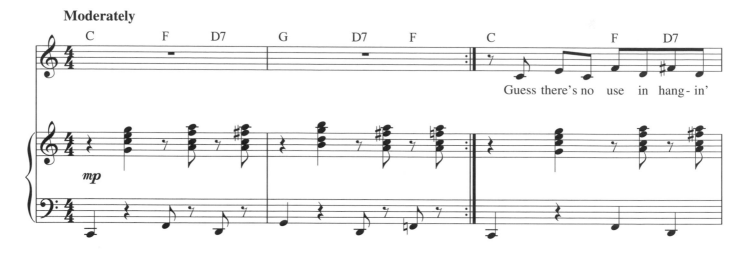

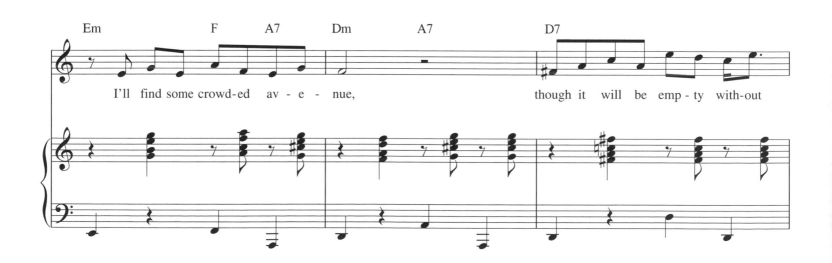

say. Since you're gone it hap - pens ev - 'ry day. ____

Can't get used to los - ing you, no mat - ter what I try to do. ____

Gon - na live my whole life through, lov - ing you. ____

lov - ing   you. _____

lov - ing   you. _____

Repeat and Fade | **Optional Ending**

molto rit.

IN THE ARMS OF LOVE

Words by RAY EVANS and JAY LIVINGSTON
Music by HENRY MANCINI

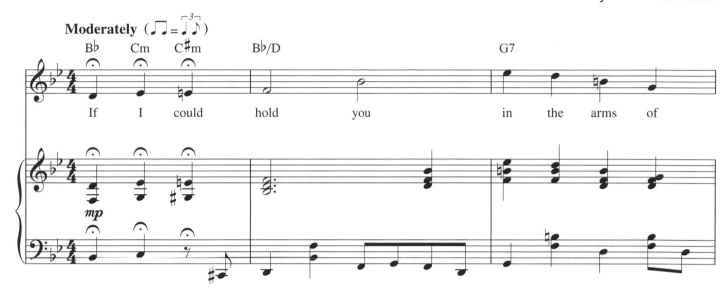

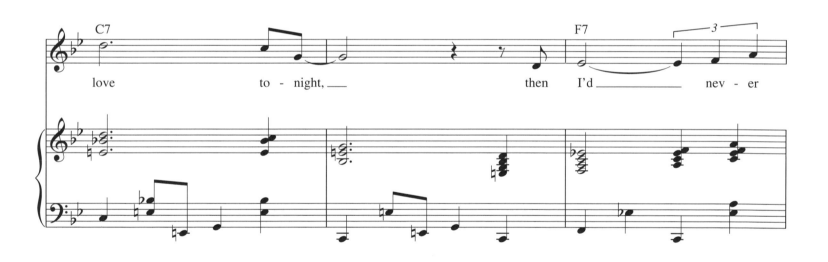

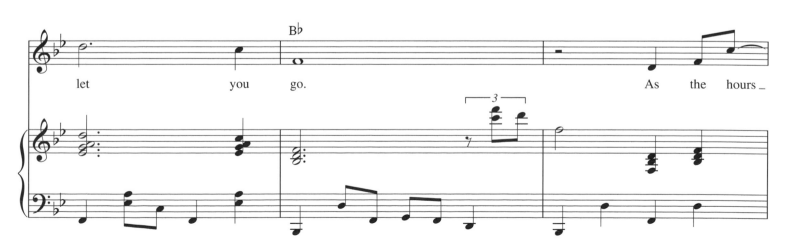

CANADIAN SUNSET

Words by NORMAN GIMBEL
Music by EDDIE HEYWOOD

DAYS OF WINE AND ROSES

Lyric by JOHNNY MERCER
Music by HENRY MANCINI

The days

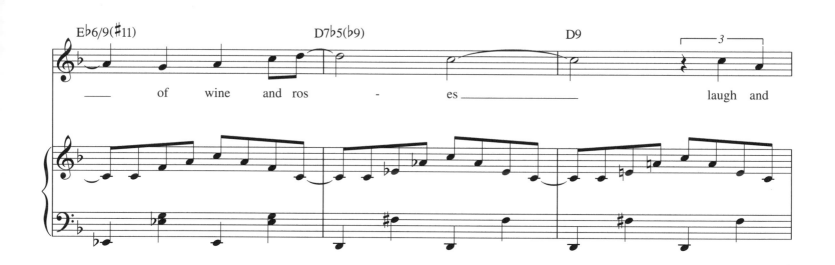

of wine and ros - es _____ laugh and

run a - way _____ like _____ a child _____ at play, _____

DEAR HEART

Music by HENRY MANCINI
Words by JAY LIVINGSTON and RAY EVANS

sin - gle room, a ta - ble for one; it's a

D.S. al Coda

lone - some town, all right.   But

CODA

arms _____ nev - er - more. _____

rit.

EMILY

Music by JOHNNY MANDEL
Words by JOHNNY MERCER

Moderately slow, in 1

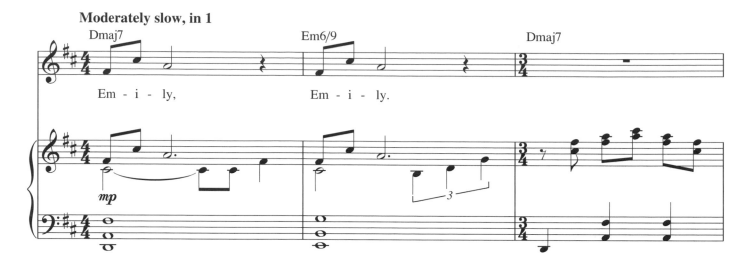

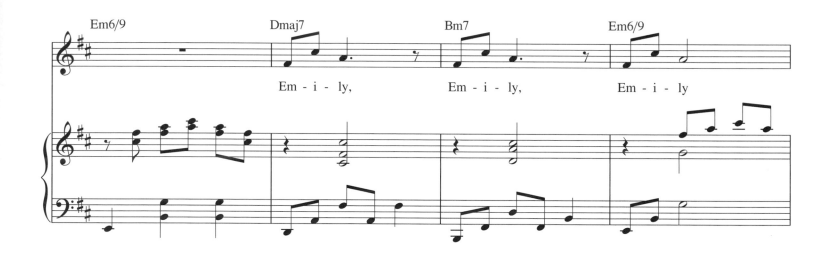

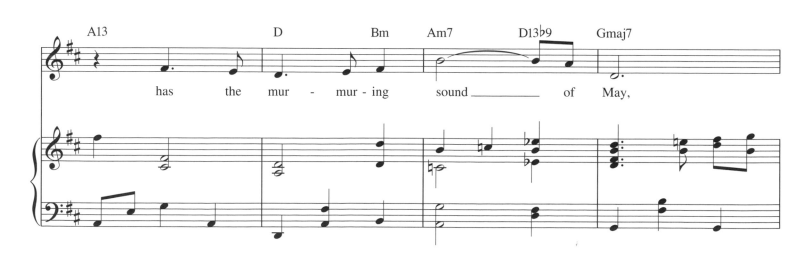

41

THE HAWAIIAN WEDDING SONG
(Ke Kali Nei Au)

English Lyrics by AL HOFFMAN
and DICK MANNING
Hawaiian Lyrics and Music by
CHARLES E. KING

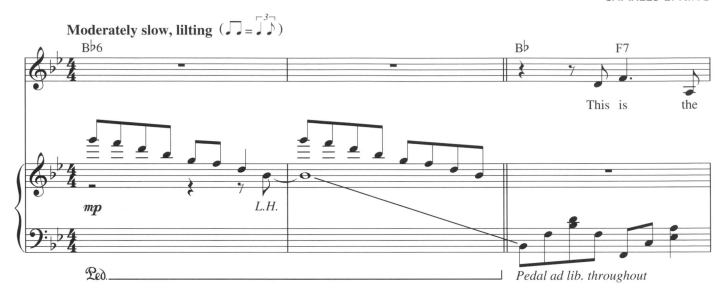

This is the

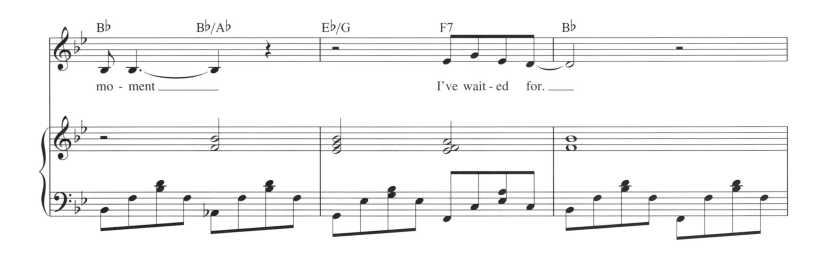

mo - ment _____ I've wait - ed for. _____

I can hear _____ my heart sing-ing; _____ soon bells will be

THE IMPOSSIBLE DREAM
(The Quest)
from MAN OF LA MANCHA

Lyric by JOE DARION
Music by MITCH LEIGH

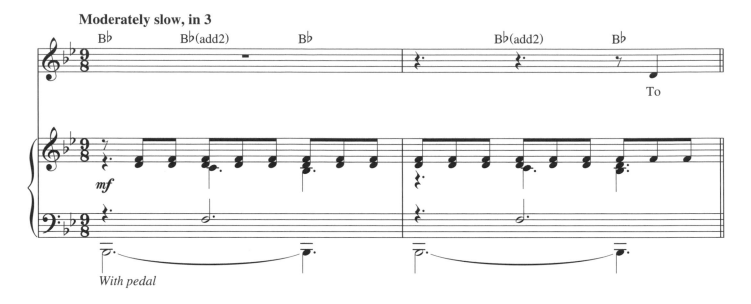

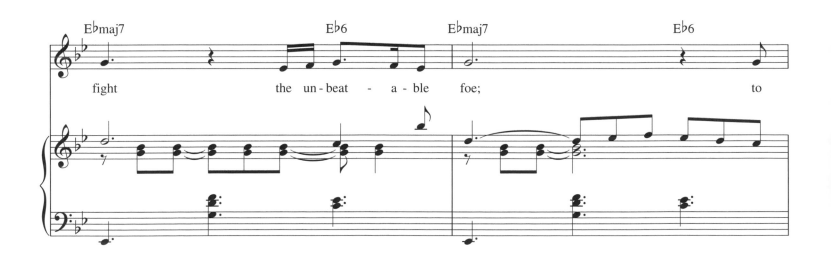

52

MARIA

from WEST SIDE STORY

Lyrics by STEPHEN SONDHEIM
Music by LEONARD BERNSTEIN

The most beau - ti - ful sound I've
ev - er heard: Ma - ri -
- a!

MAY EACH DAY

Words and Music by GEORGE WYLE
and MORT GREEN

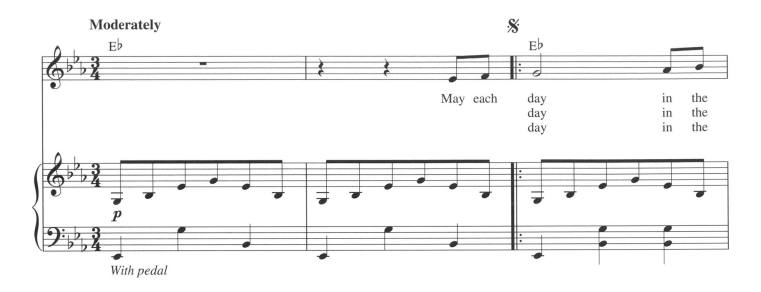

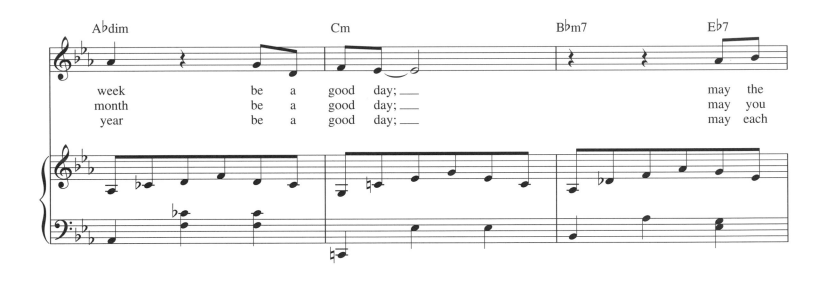

MOON RIVER
from the Paramount Picture BREAKFAST AT TIFFANY'S

Words by JOHNNY MERCER
Music by HENRY MANCINI

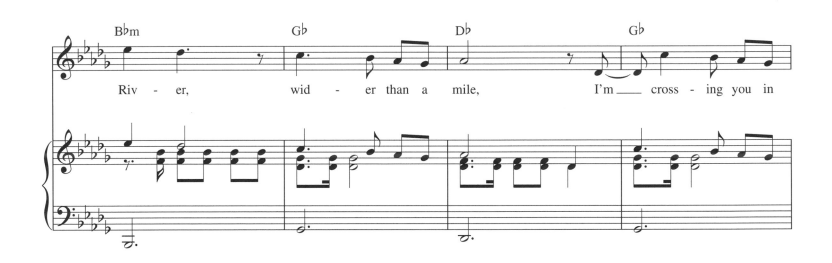

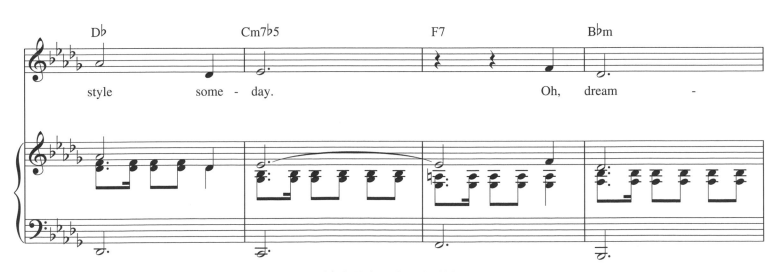

MORE
(Ti Guarderò Nel Cuore)
from the film MONDO CANE

Music by NINO OLIVIERO and RIZ ORTOLANI
Italian Lyrics by MARCELLO CIORCIOLINI
English Lyrics by NORMAN NEWELL

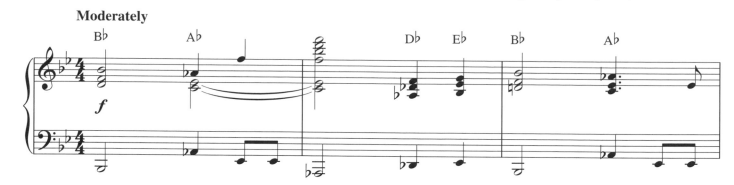

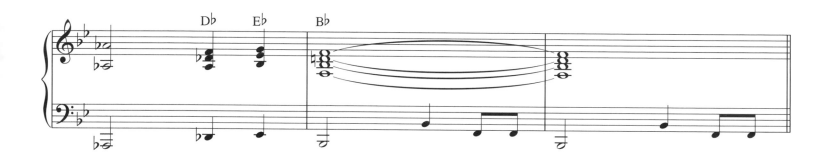

More than the great-est love the world has known, this is the love I'll give to

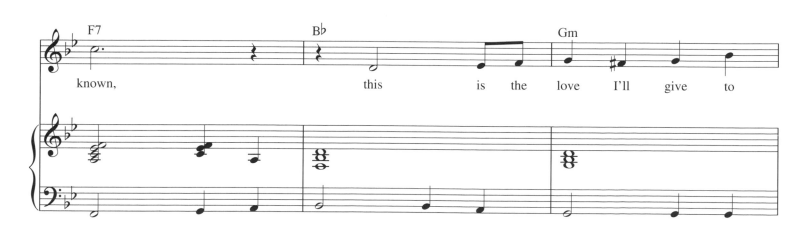

known,

THE MOST WONDERFUL
TIME OF THE YEAR

Words and Music by EDDIE POLA
and GEORGE WYLE

There'll be much mis-tle - toe - ing and hearts will be

glow - ing when loved ones are near. _____

It's the most won - der - ful time,

it's the most won - der - ful time,

RED ROSES FOR A BLUE LADY

Words and Music by SID TEPPER
and ROY C. BENNETT

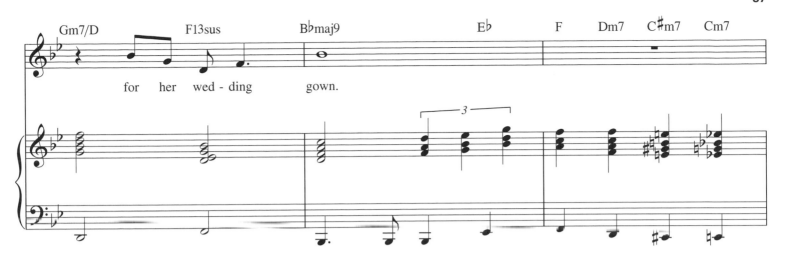

for her wed-ding gown.

And if they do the

A TIME FOR US
(Love Theme)
from the Paramount Picture ROMEO AND JULIET

Words by LARRY KUSIK and EDDIE SNYDER
Music by NINO ROTA

me. A time for us, at last, to see a life worth-while for you and me. And with our love, through tears and thorns, we will en -

SPEAK SOFTLY, LOVE
(Love Theme)
from the Paramount Picture THE GODFATHER

Words by LARRY KUSIK
Music by NINO ROTA

Speak soft-ly, love, _____ and hold me warm a-gainst your heart. I feel your words, the ten-der, trem-bling mo-ment

so soft - ly, love. _____

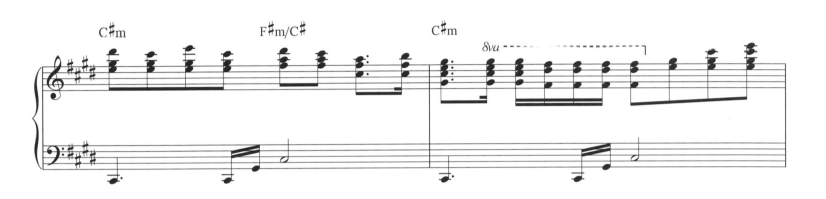

VILLAGE OF ST. BERNADETTE

Words and Music by
EULA PARKER

Lyrics:
(Ah, _____ ah.) _____

I've trav-eled far, the
Now, I am home; I'm

104

WHERE DO I BEGIN
(Love Theme)
from the Paramount Picture LOVE STORY

Words by CARL SIGMAN
Music by FRANCIS LAI

Where do I be-gin _____ to tell _____ the sto-ry of how

great a love _____ can be, the sweet love sto-ry that is old-